Original title:
Prickly Prose

Copyright © 2025 Creative Arts Management OÜ
All rights reserved.

Author: Dante Kingsley
ISBN HARDBACK: 978-1-80566-679-0
ISBN PAPERBACK: 978-1-80566-964-7

Shrubs of Dissonance

In gardens where the weeds conspire,
A dandelion plays with fire.
The roses laugh, quite out of tune,
While sunflowers dance beneath the moon.

The thorns may poke, yet still we laugh,
As crickets hum in cactus craft.
The blooms all bicker in colorful hues,
Too loud to hide their silly views.

Tangles of Truth

Twisted vines speak in riddles,
As snakes pretend to be fiddle diddles.
Each leaf a story, each stem a lie,
While owls hoot their surprise goodbye.

Yet laughter blooms amidst the fuss,
As bees create their honeyed fuss.
The truth gets stuck in bushes thick,
But humor pricks with a funny tick.

Syringe of Satire

In a garden full of puns and jibes,
A cactus winks at its funny tribes.
With needles sharp yet smiles bright,
It jabs at all, though not in spite.

A drip of wit from petals' edge,
As bumblebees make a playful pledge.
To poke and prod with a gentle jest,
In leafy realms where laughter's best.

A Hedge of Humor

Behind the hedge where jokes reside,
The squirrels gather, swiping pride.
They chuckle at the snails so slow,
While mushrooms giggle, putting on a show.

The foliage whispers secrets sweet,
Of silly tales that can't be beat.
A punchline blooms in every nook,
As nature writes its own funny book.

Shadows of the Thornbush

In the shadow of a thornbush,
Lies a tale of a hedgehog's rush.
He tried to hug, the branches said,
'Bow before us, or scratch your head!'

With spiky words, he made his case,
But left the party with an angry face.
His friends all laughed, they had their fun,
While he rolled home, the lonely one.

Thorns of Expression

Words can dance, but watch your step,
In a garden where the thorns adept.
One slip of tongue could lead to tears,
As floral friends swap blooming jeers.

A poet once wrote with zest and glee,
But found his rhymes too sharp, oh me!
He penned a verse, man's folly struck,
And every line was pure bad luck!

The Satirical Prick

There once was a prick from an old fairytale,
With pointed jabs, he'd surely derail.
His quips were sharp, like cactus spines,
Leaving all to question their own lines.

At the gallows of wit, he'd tilt his quill,
To pen a jest that's sure to thrill.
With every word he'd take a jab,
Making the wise cracks mare or blab!

Barbed Words

Barbed words flit on velvet breeze,
Make you chuckle, or bring you to knees.
A quip caught fire, igniting the room,
While laughter bloomed, the laughter would zoom.

A jester's crown was not all gold,
For every jest was a blow, we're told.
With a wink and a laugh, the punchline struck,
As friends would shout, 'Oh, what sheer luck!'

Bitter Ink

Bitter ink ran through my pen,
Telling tales of thorns and men.
With every drop, a laugh would leak,
As readers squirmed, unable to speak.

The parchment cringed, not quite prepared,
For words that bit, though none were scared.
In the margins, laughter grew wild,
A twist of fate, like a cheeky child.

Points of Contention

In the garden of debates, we meet,
With blooming words that can't be beat.
Each point is sharp, a thorny fest,
We banter loud, but love the jest.

The prick of laughter, oh so sweet,
As ideas dance on agile feet.
In this clash of wit, we throw,
The humor stings, but joy will grow.

A Palette of Punctures

Colorful quips upon the wall,
Each shade a jab, a hearty brawl.
We paint with humor, so divine,
A canvas bright, where laughter shines.

With splashes bold, we carve our way,
Through jesting strokes, we play all day.
Each puncture adds to the delight,
A masterpiece of laughs in sight.

Stinging Truths

Oh, the truths that tickle and sting,
Wrapped in giggles, they lightly cling.
With every jest, a lesson sly,
We watch the laughter fly up high.

In the sting of jokes, we find our place,
A truth unveiled with a silly face.
With wit as sharp as a needle's eye,
These stinging truths will never die.

Jagged Narratives

In tales where humor meets the knife,
 Stories twist, bringing them to life.
 With jagged edges, they entertain,
 Laughter dances through the pain.

Each plot's a prick, a poke, a jab,
Yet woven tight like a charming fab.
In narratives sharp, we find the grace,
 For laughter blooms in every place.

Thorns of Expression

Words spout like weeds, one or two,
Twisting and turning, but who knew?
Laughter caught in a net of wit,
Bumbling thoughts refuse to sit.

With a giggle, I pen my plight,
Sketching chaos with pure delight.
Each prick a poke, a playful jest,
In the garden where banter rests.

Jagged Lines of Thought

Thoughts like rickety fences sway,
Bumping and jostling in disarray.
When humor joins the raucous game,
It tickles the brain and sparks the flame.

Clumsy rhymes and tongues that trip,
Tangled tongues on a silly trip.
Jabs and jests in sharp relief,
Each chuckle masks a hidden grief.

Beyond the Barbs

Beneath the spines, a story hides,
Giggles squeezing through the sides.
Jokes like jelly stuck on a wall,
Bouncing back with a joyful call.

Quirky tales from twisted roots,
Witty banter in cactus suits.
Every thorn a punchline, bright,
Poking fun in soft daylight.

The Cactus Chronicles

In a desert where laughter blooms,
A cactus tells of silly rooms.
With arms so sharp but never mean,
It winks and teases, a comic scene.

Each story a twist, a laughter line,
Holding on to joy, oh so fine.
Witty barbs in a sunlit spree,
A prick with a smile, so carefree.

Needles of Insight

In a garden of ideas, oh what a mess,
The petals are jokes, but the stems—more or less.
With needles of truth poking through the fluff,
I giggle and ponder, is this deep stuff?

Every thought feels like it's got some zing,
As I stumble on words that can trip like a spring.
A bloom of bright banter, it all feels so right,
In the patch of my mind, I dance with delight.

Cuts of the Mind

With a flick of the pen, there's a sharp little cut,
Words slicing through silence, oh what a glut.
Each sentence a bandage, wrapped tight with a grin,
As laughter pours out from the chaos within.

I stitch up the stories that fray at the seams,
Mind-magic unfolding, like wild, quirky dreams.
With each clever jab, I'm unraveling tight,
In this circus of thoughts, I'm the ringmaster's bite!

The Resilience of Rhetoric

Oh, the power of words that bounce and they twirl,
They poke and they jab, oh what a wild whirl!
With wit that can thwart all the gloom in the air,
Each pun like a miracle, the laughter we share.

Rhetoric's gentle needle weaves tales full of cheer,
Crafting thoughts into stitches, each quip crystal clear.
In the fabric of chatter, we twine and we twist,
Creating a canvas of smiles that persist.

Gleaming Thorns

In a rose bush of musings, sharp bits abound,
Each thorn hides a jest that's delightfully sound.
As I pluck at the petals, laughter's the prize,
Finding joy in the stabs hidden deep in disguise.

With gleaming thorns shining in broad daylight,
Each prick brings a giggle, a tickle, a bite.
We dance through the garden of thoughts sharp and keen,
In this merry patch of wit, we reign as the queen!

Bristle and Bloom

In the garden of sass, a plant takes the stage,
With thorns all around, it's a prickly age.
"Come near for a hug!" it cheery insists,
But one sharp glance says, "That's not on my list!"

Fluffy petals laugh, sporting armor so bold,
They giggle at bees who are slightly too bold.
"Buzz off, little fella! You've come to the wrong!"
They twirl with the sun, all too proud of their song!

Stinging Verses

Words dance with delight, like a cactus on fire,
Each line has a jab that may spark your desire.
"Read on, if you dare!" they gleefully tease,
But watch for the pricks, not all are a breeze!

Underneath layers, where secrets reside,
The humor is sharp, yet it becomes a good ride.
"Hey, you might just bleed, if you tread here too deep!"
Chuckle with caution, take the leap or just creep!

The Art of Spikes

The canvas is rough, a masterpiece drawn,
With spikes that emerge from the light of the dawn.
Each stroke is a smile, each prickle a jest,
In the garden of humor, the art's not at rest.

Every thorn tells a tale, it's a curious thing,
How laughter and pain can waltz in the spring.
So grab your paintbrush and come join the spree,
But be mindful of splinters, they sting, oh, they be!

Spiny Reflections

In the mirror of wit, a reflection appears,
A spiny extravaganza that tickles your fears.
"Oh snap!" says the glare, with a laughter so sly,
"Don't lean in too close, or you just might cry!"

With each prickly jest, there's a glimmer of glee,
They pull at your edges, demanding to see.
The more that you chuckle, the sharper they grow,
In a world full of thorns, don't forget to sow!

Bursting Buds of Dissent

In the garden of talk, petals unfurl,
Tiny voices rise, hopes in a whirl.
Yet butting heads with stubborn stems,
Oh, the laughter that springs from their gems!

Pollen of chaos drifts through the air,
Each word a bee, buzzing without a care.
With humor so bright, they jostle and tease,
A riot of blooms swaying in the breeze.

A Hedge of Irony

Behind a green wall, truths play peek-a-boo,
Witty barbs dodging the skies so blue.
They prickle and poke, this sly little hedge,
With laughter and teasing, it won't let you pledge.

Each leaf a quip, each branch a jest,
Who would have thought irony can jest?
As we trim the edges, the jokes can provoke,
A runway of humor wrapped in pure cloak.

Wounds in the Stanza

Words sting and scratch, they're oh so bold,
Dancing on verses, stories unfold.
Each line, a bandage with a twist of fate,
Healing the prose with a chuckle, not hate.

In rhymes, little cuts start to bleed,
Blunders that happen are part of the creed.
Laughing at faces all bruised in the fray,
The beauty of blunders makes fun of the day.

Thorns of the Mind

Thoughts like thorns can poke and prod,
Twisting the tales we weave and nod.
A mental bouquet bursting with glee,
As laughter erupts from the thistles, you see!

Each prick a reminder of lessons to learn,
Jokes grow wild, watch their flames brightly burn.
In the garden of wit, we sprout and sway,
Witty little thorns, come join the ballet!

Points of Contemplation

In a world full of thorns, we gather,
Laughter echoing, light as a feather.
Thoughts dart like hedgehogs on the go,
Searching for meaning in a comic show.

Pondering jokes that make no sense,
Life's riddles wrapped in a humorous fence.
Twisting and turning, minds in a knot,
Finding the wit in the tangled thought.

Each chuckle sharpens the wit within,
As we wrestle with life, a playful spin.
We bloom even with arrows in our back,
In jest, we thrive; that's our quirky knack.

So gather 'round, friends, don't be shy,
Let's laugh at the pricks as we pass them by.
In humor's embrace, let's dance and play,
In points of contemplation, we'll find our way.

Barbed Words

Words can sting like a bee on a spree,
But wrapped in laughter, they set us free.
We jab and poke with clever intent,
Each barbed quip is a playful sent.

In meetings of minds, we hear the clatter,
Witty repartees, oh what a matter!
With barbs so sharp, yet sweetly spun,
We sail through life, laughing, having fun.

Caught in a web of clever exchanges,
In the land of puns, joy rearranges.
Wit is our armor, humor our shield,
With barbed words, our laughter is revealed.

So let's trade jests like other folks trade stocks,
In this wild journey, there's plenty of knocks.
With every jab, our spirits will soar,
In the realm of banter, who could ask for more?

The Beauty of Scratches

Scratches on skin tell tales of the past,
Every little mark, a memory cast.
With laughter, we share these jagged tales,
In humor's embrace, our spirit prevails.

Dancing through life with laughter's delight,
We twist and turn, both day and night.
Each scrape a trophy, we wear with pride,
In the game of living, we take it all in stride.

Beauty lies not in a flawless sheen,
But in the quirks that our lives have seen.
Embracing the mess, we shine through the grime,
In this patchwork of laughs, we find our rhyme.

So raise a glass to the stories we share,
To the scratches of life that show we dare.
In the beauty of flaws, our laughter ignites,
A colorful canvas that endlessly excites.

Jagged Journeys

We wander on paths that twist and dive,
With jagged edges, we learn to thrive.
Each step a giggle, each turn a jest,
In this chaotic dance, we feel so blessed.

With each stumble, we find our grace,
In the slapstick journey, we pick up the pace.
Laughter our compass as we trek this land,
Finding joy in the bumps, life's quirky brand.

The road is rough, full of ups and downs,
Yet in our smiles, we wear no frowns.
We laugh at the hurdles that life has spun,
In jagged journeys, together, we run.

So here's to the twists that make us whole,
To the jagged paths that pull at our soul.
With laughter as fuel, we journey afar,
In the crazy ride of life, we shine like a star.

Hurdles of Dialogue

Words leap like frogs, so spry,
Each hop a chance to fly.
I trace my thoughts with care,
Yet they twist like tangled hair.

Every word a daring feat,
Some land soft, some take a seat.
Conversations dance in circles tight,
I nod and grin, in awkward delight.

Like a game of hopscotch played,
With every blunder, I'm dismayed.
Yet laughter bubbles under skin,
These hurdles keep us wearing thin.

When words collide, sparks ignite,
I trip, I fall, but take flight.
For in this chaos, wisdom lies,
With every slip, we still can rise.

Wounds that Speak

Every jab, a tale to tell,
In clumsy chats, I often dwell.
With each hot take, I draw a sigh,
My heart it bleeds, but oh, I try.

I wear my scars like fancy clothes,
Each blemish blooms, a comical pose.
Reflections back, like mirror cracks,
These wounds, they giggle, share the flaks.

In battles fought with flared replies,
I find the humor in all the lies.
Through gritted teeth, I find a laugh,
My pain a punchline on life's draft.

So let them speak, the cuts and scrapes,
In every scar, a glee escapes.
With laughter's balm, we mend the seams,
For wounds that speak, ignite our dreams.

The Tangle of Sentences

Words weave a web, quite a sight,
Like spaghetti at a dinner fight.
I search for clarity, oh what a jest,
These sentences tangle, fail the test.

Like cats in a box, they twist and turn,
Each phrase a flame, but none can burn.
A riddle tossed in a zany stew,
Unravel, unravel, oh where's the clue?

With every comma, confusion reigns,
Like trying to dance on runaway trains.
Yet in the mess, a spark may flare,
A jest, a giggle, we share the air.

So laugh along with this silly game,
In tangled words, we feel the same.
For in the mayhem, friendships grow,
The joy of chaos, on we flow.

Frayed Edges of Meaning

When thoughts unspool like yarn gone wild,
And meanings crumble, havoc styled.
I grasp at threads, oh how they slip,
These frayed edges, a comic trip.

In every point, a twist or bend,
I search for sense, around the bend.
But laughter lingers in each mistake,
For clarity's sake, let's take a break.

Ideas clash like pots and pans,
Bouncing off with awkward plans.
But in the chaos, surprise awaits,
A chuckle blooms as humor creates.

So let us cherish this silly strife,
In fragments, we find the zest of life.
With frayed edges, we craft a tale,
In jest we sail, we cannot fail.

Twisted Meadows

In the meadow of mash-ups, winds dance and twist,
Where daisies wear glasses, they can't resist.
The sun's a goofy jester with a wink and a flare,
Tickling the daisies with its bright golden hair.

A rabbit hops by, tripping over a shoe,
He's models in fashion, with a dazzling view.
The grass giggles loud, with secrets it hides,
As squirrels make bets on the height of their rides.

Petunias gossip like busy old maids,
While thistles and thorns plan their hilarious parades.
"Who wore it best?" they chuckle and cheer,
As butterflies bat their lashes, all haughty, all near.

This land is a riddle wrapped in a rhyme,
Where humor grows freely, just biding its time.
Every bloom a punchline, each stalk a delight,
In Twisted Meadows, the laughter takes flight.

Defiant Flowers

In a world full of weeds, here come the bold blooms,
They flaunt their bright colors, banishing glooms.
With petals like shields and a fragrance so snappy,
Defiant they stand, never meek, never sappy.

The sunflowers salute with an army of cheer,
While daisies declare, "We have nothing to fear!"
A wild rose whispers, "Join the fun clout,
Who said they'd keep us down? Let's dance it all out!"

Lily pods giggle under the mischievous sky,
While dandelions puff up, grinning wide and spry.
Every thorn is a badge of their wit and their pride,
In the face of the norm, they refuse to abide.

Defiant flowers raise their voices in song,
Let humor be the anthem where they all belong.
With petals like banners, they turn trials to jest,
In a garden of laughter, they flourish and rest.

Cacti in Bloom

In the land of the spiky, where the boldness is bright,
Cacti wear smiles, an odd, funny sight.
With arms raised in laughter, they greet every guest,
As they bloom into colors, a comedic fest.

Prickles and humor, a curious mix,
Each cactus a character, a garden of tricks.
The ocotillo wiggles, doing a dance,
While saguaro jokes with a cheeky romance.

In the sun-drenched oasis, the laughter takes hold,
With humor as fierce as the desert, so bold.
The lizards all chuckle, they can't help but tease,
As they bask in the warmth of the spiky spree.

Cacti stand tall, with glee they exclaim,
"Who needs softness? We're proud of our name!"
In this blooming kingdom of jesters and beams,
The prickles just sparkle, the humor redeems.

Staccato of Snags

Life has its snags, says the thistle with flair,
With a chuckle it grips what no one would dare.
Each snag tells a story, a poke and a jab,
It's a staccato of laughter wrapped in a cab.

The brambles are rascals, with tales to unfold,
Of all the mischief in fields of pure gold.
They snicker and snort as they tangle and twine,
In the rhythm of nature, it's all quite divine.

Barbed wires play harmonies, sharp as a quill,
While the laughing grass chimes with a whimsical thrill.
Every snag's a note in this quirky old song,
With each little prick, oh, the laughter's so strong!

In the gardens of jests where the misfits all meet,
There's humor in hazards, each thorny defeat.
So embrace all the snags, let the fun firmly cling,
In the staccato of life, let the laughter take wing!

Thoughts Like Briars

In a garden of thoughts, they do grow,
Twisting and turning, stealing the show.
Each jab a reminder, of brambles and thorns,
Lurking in shadows, where mischief is born.

I ponder my puns, sharp as a knife,
Prickling my brain, oh, what a life!
They dance in my head, these ideas so sly,
Bouncing and buzzing, like bees in July.

With giggles they creep, taking form and flight,
Jokes on the cusp, ready to ignite.
Yet tangled and twisted, they sometimes collide,
A joke and a jab, in a tangled ride.

So here's to the thorns, the witty and wild,
Turning the mundane into a child.
In a world full of thicket, let laughter ring true,
For even the prickly can tickle you too.

Bitter Sweet Syntax

Words weave together, a tapestry bright,
With threads of sweet humor, stitched wrong and right.
Each phrase a puzzle, cryptic and neat,
Tripping on syllables, oh, such a feat!

The bittersweet taste of language we chew,
With twists like a vine that just won't break through.
Syntax a jester, plays tricks on my mind,
Crafting conundrums, one of a kind.

I stumble on phrases, they poke and they prod,
Like rogue little fairies, giving me nods.
Their playful enchantments bring back a smile,
As I navigate language, mile after mile.

So let's toast to the blend of delight and despair,
In a banquet of words, let's strip down the flair.
For in every misstep, a chuckle can sprout,
Bitter sweet syntax, let's laugh it all out!

The Chisel of Diction

With a chisel of diction, I carve out the words,
Sharp angles of humor, like trolls and their herds.
Each chuckle a chip off the block of my thought,
Crafting a sentence, with laughter well-sought.

I sculpt out the wit, from stony discourse,
Words tumble and roll, like a prize-winning horse.
The shaping of phrases, a whimsical feat,
Where the sharp meets the silly, the bitter, the sweet.

As I hammer away at the structure and form,
Whittling away at the norm's dreary storm.
In this quirky workshop, where ideas collide,
My chisel brings forth, laughter inside.

So let's chip away, in this playful embrace,
For in every sharp turn, there's a smile on each face.
With a chisel in hand, and a grin to behold,
Crafting the funny, as the stories unfold!

Braided Barbs

In a tangle of tales, they twist and they weave,
Barbed humor dances, so hard to believe.
Each quip a thorn, each jest a tight braid,
In the harvest of laughter, together they're laid.

With snickers and giggles, the stories unwind,
Like strands of bright yarn, differently signed.
Braiding together the sharp and the fun,
In this quirky abode, where silliness runs.

I chuckle at jabs, so sprightly and sly,
Barbed wit is a treasure, oh me, oh my!
Each poke and each prod, a tickle in jest,
In a garden of humor, we're humor's best guest.

So gather the barbs, entwined in delight,
For laughter's a journey, let's savor the flight.
In the maze of our minds, rich with light and dark,
Braided barbs bring laughter; let's ignite that spark!

Sharp Tongues and Sweet Sorrows

In the land where words collide,
Tongues flick like blades side to side.
Sarcasm sings a merry tune,
While laughter wafts beneath the moon.

Sweet sorrows spill from every quip,
Life's absurdities make us flip.
With every jab, we giggle more,
In shades of wit, we explore the shore.

Cutting remarks, a playful sport,
We jest, we tease—who needs retort?
Life's a comedy of sharp delight,
In whirling words, we take our flight.

So bring your thorns, we dance and play,
These jagged edges brighten our day.
Through the thicket of jests, we'll roam,
Finding joy in this wordy home.

Echoes of the Gritty Quill

A quill in hand, a tale to tell,
Ink spills like laughter, oh so well.
With gritty strokes, the stories flow,
Fables tinged with humor's glow.

Each sentence dances, sharp and sweet,
Where woes and whims delight to meet.
The pages crinkle, laughter shrieks,
In the echoes, truth lightly peaks.

Grit hangs heavy, yet hearts take flight,
Words like featherweights, oh what a sight!
With clever twists and comical bends,
We pen our lives, where laughter blends.

So let the quills scratch on and on,
Through every jest, we find the dawn.
With echoes ringing, spirits soar,
In the gritty rhyme, we ask for more.

The Prick of Awareness

Awareness pricks like a tiny thorn,
From slumbering minds, new thoughts are born.
A giggle slips from sharp delight,
As light dawns heavy on the night.

We face the absurd with elegant flair,
In blunders grand, we find our dare.
Wit sharpens edges, prompts a snort,
In every folly, a snazzy report.

A laugh erupts, the steam it spills,
Amid the pricks of everyday thrills.
Like bubbles burst in a wild dance,
Our aware hearts embrace the chance.

So tread lightly on this spiny path,
We'll navigate with joyous wrath.
For every prick that life can lend,
Awareness brings a quirky friend.

Barbed Narratives

In tales where barbs kiss the air,
Laughter mingles with threads of despair.
Each narrative, a thorny embrace,
Woven tight with humor's grace.

Barbed narratives twist and turn,
From raucous jests, our hearts do learn.
With each sharp edge, a fact revealed,
The truth in laughter, joyous and healed.

Words with stingers, yet soft as breeze,
Tickling minds, like playful tease.
We dance in shadows of sharp delight,
Finding gold in the prickly night.

So gather round, let's share these tales,
Of barbs and giggles that never fail.
In narratives where our spirits ignite,
The humor shines, forever bright.

The Jagged Tongue

Words as sharp as a cactus' spine,
They dance and prance, like they're divine.
With every jab, a laugh is found,
In the garden of wit, we're all unwound.

My sentences twist, they poke and tease,
Like a porcupine in a gentle breeze.
I spew my thoughts without a care,
Tongue in cheek, truth laid bare.

Every not-so-smooth phrase I speak,
Adds to the humor, makes the day a peek.
Sharp edges bring the fun to the table,
Wit unfiltered, and that's the fable.

So let the jagged tongue have its say,
In the tangled mess, we find our play.
With each barb, the laughter grows,
Life's too short for dull prose.

Sharp Sentiments

In a world of blunts, I wield my knife,
Carving insights with a joy for life.
Each sentiment cuts, but with a grin,
The sharper the jab, the more we win.

I wear my heart on a thorny sleeve,
Making folks chuckle, just watch them heave.
Witty barbs are my arsenal bright,
In jest, I find my pure delight.

Twist and turn, the laughter flows,
With every prick, our joy just grows.
A little sting adds flavor anew,
In this garden of words, I nurture the few.

So let's toast to the sharp and the sly,
Where humor and truth always lie.
For in every cut, a story is spun,
To wield sharp sentiments, oh what fun!

Thorned Reflections

In the mirror of wit, faces show,
Reflections of humor, with thorns in tow.
Each laugh a tickle, each poke a tease,
In this garden, our hearts feel at ease.

Oh, look at the flowers, what a sight!
But beware, the thorns give a little fright.
With every chuckle, there's a little sting,
In thorned reflections, we find our zing.

Dancing around the pricks of fate,
Every jab we take, we celebrate.
Life's a comedy, sharp and bright,
In thorns, we find our sheer delight.

So gather 'round, let the laughter ring,
Let's toast to the thorns that jokes can bring.
In thorned reflections, we shine our best,
Finding joy amid the jest.

The Harsh Elegy

In the quiet room, I raise a glass,
To the words we wield like a prickly mass.
With every harsh line, laughter unfurls,
A melody of stabs, in this dance of pearls.

Elegy of jest, a tribute sung,
To the sharper moments, where laughter sprung.
With every bite, we find our tune,
In humor's embrace, we gather the boon.

Though words may sting, we treasure their chime,
In the harshest of tones, we find the rhyme.
So let's not mourn but cherish the quirks,
In this elegy steeped in mirthful perks.

Raise your voice and let it ring,
For the funny times and the joy we bring.
In harsh elegies, beauty is spun,
As laughter ignites, we're never done.

Jagged Edge of Verses

Words cut like a cactus thorn,
And yet their bloom can leave you worn.
A jolly jest, a sharpened quip,
A chuckle's ease, a mindful trip.

With every jest, a brief surprise,
In humor's shade, the laughter lies.
So tread with care, and mind your talk,
Or else you'll find a giggle's rock.

When sentences curve and twist about,
Like winding paths we laugh and shout.
Each jagged phrase, a wondrous leap,
A ticklish tangle, fun to keep.

So join the dance, embrace the jest,
In jagged forms, we find our best.
A verse, a laugh, a friendly poke,
On jagged edges, words evoke.

Cactus Whispers

In the desert where the giggles grow,
Watch out for spines in the afterglow.
With every laugh, a prickly tease,
It's humor's charm, like summer breeze.

The cactus speaks in quiet tones,
With witty words, it laughs alone.
A prick here, a poke there, it plays,
Whispering jokes throughout the days.

Bound by spines, it tells a tale,
Of bubbling joy that cannot fail.
So pluck your wit from thorny ground,
In chortled whispers, smiles abound.

Through prickles sharp, the joy will flow,
In laughter's grip, we come to grow.
So heed the call of cactus fun,
With every laugh, we've surely won.

Serrated Lines of Thought

Thoughts may slice with serrated edge,
Yet in their cut, we find a pledge.
To laugh out loud, embrace the jest,
In every line, humor's the best.

Each sentence twists, a wild affair,
In jagged forms, we find our bear.
A thought so sharp, it pricks the mind,
Yet in the jest, pure joy we find.

With every stutter, whimsy reigns,
In jagged edges, laughter gains.
So tiptoe 'round those slicing words,
And find the fun amidst the birds.

In serrated verses, joy takes flight,
Where wit and charm meet day and night.
So dance along these tricky rhymes,
And savor every laugh that climbs.

Spines of Language

Language has its spines, we know,
With every poke, a laugh can grow.
In witticisms, we take our aim,
Defining humor's playful game.

A spine can tickle, or make one squirm,
With every word, the giggles worm.
So choose your phrasing with some care,
Lest you incur a prickly flare.

Through tangled metaphors, we wade,
In laughter's orchard, pranks are made.
Transformed by quips, we find our way,
In sharp exchanges, we laugh and play.

So twist your tongue and poke the fun,
In spines of language, we are one.
Amusing tales from thorns of thought,
In every line, a giggle caught.

The Sharpest Pencil

There once was a pencil, shiny and bright,
It claimed it could write with all of its might.
But when it met paper, it started to slip,
A dance of disaster; what a wild trip!

Its lead would then shatter with just one hard poke,
Leaving letters jagged like a badly cracked yolk.
Yet giggles would bubble when mistakes would appear,
For laughter's a joy that can conquer all fear.

In the drawer it would sit, proud of its fame,
Its story included in an awkward game.
With wit like a razor and style like a fool,
This pencil's sharp antics broke every old rule!

So here's to the scribbles that never went right,
To the joy of the journey, the shade of delight.
With humor as ink, let your thoughts dance and play,
For life's just a canvas; doodle away!

The Nail-Biting Diction

In the land of the letters, where grammar's the king,
Lived a word that would cause quite a nail-biting fling.
With syllables scary and tenses all wrong,
It giggled and wiggled, a mischievous song!

The verbs would protest, 'This just isn't fair!'
While adverbs held their breath, caught up in despair.
But nouns found it funny, oh what a great laugh,
As they watched the wild syntax try to split in half!

A punctuation party erupted that day,
With commas and periods leading the fray.
Exclamation points danced, what a bouncing affair,
While question marks teased, "Let's just leave it a dare!"

Through poetic chaos, the laughter would flow,
As diction unraveled in its comic show.
Next time you scribble, let your words take a leap,
For behind all the chaos, new treasures we reap!

Grit and Grace

There once was a fighter, tough as can be,
With grit in their heart and a mind filled with glee.
But each time they spoke, a giggle was found,
Their words would tumble and roll on the ground!

They'd quote all the classics with mischief and cheer,
Turning solemn phrases to something unclear.
With a twist and a turn, their tongue danced around,
Making Shakespeare trip on the lines that they found!

When it came to the challenge, they'd swagger and boast,

Yet their punchlines would land like a bad ghost's toast.
Though tough as a boulder, with flaws on display,
Their grit wrapped in grace made it all seem okay!

So raise up your glasses to those who can trip,
With words like confetti, they revel and skip.
In laughter, we find that true strength can ignite,
As we dance through the shadows, painting wrongs into right!

An Incision of Words

Words could be daggers, sharp and unkind,
Yet in jests they blossom, so hilariously blind.
With each little quip, and a punchline well-timed,
What was once just a cut, now humor's entwined!

A slice of good laughter, a witty retort,
Those stabs of delight, they muddle with sport.
As the audience chuckles, they just can't resist,
The art of the incision becomes hard to miss.

From the corners of jokes where sarcasm gleams,
To one-liners sharp like a swordsman's dreams.
Each cut finds its mark, a playful parade,
As laughter ricochets through the jokes we've made!

So wield your sharp words like a jester's grand knife,
Make cuts that bring joy, and celebrate life.
For in every incision, let guffaws take flight,
And turn every ouch into purest delight!

Cacti in the Mind's Eye

In the garden of my dreams, they grow,
A thousand thoughts that poke and flow.
With a smile, I tread on this bumpy path,
    A tickle of wit, a quirky laugh.

Those spines are sharp, yet oh so grand,
    Ideas dance in a fevered band.
Each prick a spark, each stab a jest,
In this weird world, I am the guest.

So gather 'round, my jolly crew,
Let's embrace the odd with a giggle or two.
In the mind's eye, where joy takes flight,
    Cacti bloom in the dead of night.

With laughter's balm, let's buffer the sting,
    For within this thicket, joy takes wing.
Through twisted paths of jumbled thought,
    A garden of wit, freshly wrought.

Words That Stab

My pen's a knife, oh how it jives,
With every poke, a laugh arrives.
A quip, a jab, a snarky line,
In this crazy script, I intertwine.

Each phrase a point, and sharp it seems,
I scribble down my wildest dreams.
In jests and jabs, the humor's key,
Like an ant biting a tree.

With witty blades, I carve the air,
Laughing at life, without a care.
In every cut, there's a chuckle near,
Words that stab, bring hearty cheer.

So join the fray with joyous flair,
Let's dance on edges without a scare.
In the realm of phrases, we thrive and sway,
With laughter's shine, we'll weave our play.

The Satirist's Thorn

A satirist's pen, a thorny stake,
It pricks with truth, makes no mistake.
Each poke reveals a jolly plight,
In shadows, laughter ignites the light.

With sharp-tongued glee, I navigate,
Through tangled tales that fascinate.
Mirth in the madness, wit in the fight,
A dance with irony, pure delight.

Wielding my words like thorns of jest,
I capture rapture in every quest.
With laughter wrapped around my heart,
The satirist's thorn is a work of art.

So read my riffs, let chuckles flow,
In this thorny maze, we all will grow.
Where humor blooms and troubles fade,
In the garden of wit, we're not afraid.

Thicket of Thought

In the thicket where ideas cling,
Thoughts collide, bounce, and spring.
A jungle of puns, sharp as can be,
Twisting and turning, wild and free.

Each branch a quirk, each bush a tease,
A riot of whimsy, if you please.
With laughter's breeze rustling leaves,
In this mental garden, no one grieves.

Chasing shadows of whimsical beams,
In tangled laughter, we weave our dreams.
With sharp-edged fun, let's paint the day,
In the thicket of thought, let's laugh and play.

So wander through this playful maze,
Where humor sprouts in myriad ways.
In every prickle, a smile will bloom,
In this joyful haunt, we're free to zoom.

Spiked Verses Among Roses

In a garden where humor blooms,
Laughter tickles as each petal looms.
We dance with spines, a waltz so bold,
While storytelling thorns share secrets untold.

Jokes sprout from branches, oh what a sight,
Puns like pollen, taking flight.
With every jab, a chuckle so sweet,
Each prick of laughter, a prickly treat.

Roses roll their eyes, yet join the jest,
Wrapped in banter, they feel so blessed.
Planting smiles amidst the sharp,
Cracking up, with nature's harp.

As blooms burst forth, mischief runs wild,
Wit and wonder come to be styled.
In this thorny patch, merriment holds,
Crafting chuckles as the story unfolds.

The Thorny Tragedy

A cactus crowd at a comedy night,
With painful punchlines that take flight.
Each quip like a needle, sharp and bright,
Leaving the audience in stitches despite the plight.

Three prickled pals take the stage,
Telling tales of love in a thorny cage.
"Why don't we hug?" One asks in despair,
"Because dear friend, we'll need a repair!"

Laughter erupts, so absurdly clear,
As barbs begin to disappear.
Humor's the salve for each jagged tale,
In the end, it's smiles that prevail.

Through thorns and trouble, the jesters beam,
In a world where laughter reigns supreme.
Join the ruckus, let the fun ignite,
For even a thorn can lighten the night.

Cuts That Cut Deep

Caution advised when sharing tales,
For humor can sting, and laughter fails.
A comedy club of spines and chains,
Where each joke slices, and nothing remains.

The first act stung, they just couldn't cope,
With puns as sharp as a sliver of hope.
One jest leaves scars that laughter won't heal,
But oh, the fun of a comedic wheel!

Through gales of giggles, they take the plunge,
Cutting each other with jokes that lunge.
When life gets rough and thorns crowd near,
Just laugh it off, shed a jovial tear.

The final act bows, leaving us sore,
As cuts that cut deep, lead us to roar.
In this world of jagged delights,
The more we laugh, the brighter our sights.

The Jagged Heartbeat

In a world of laughter, a heart beats rough,
Where jokes fly like arrows, sharp yet tough.
With every punchline, a startled start,
A jagged rhythm, the essence of art.

Silly tales of love's bitter kiss,
Where every barb hides a hit-or-miss.
Romance and humor, a thorny pair,
Finding joy in cuts and despair.

Their hearts beat together, rhythm unkempt,
Dancing through thorns as laughter exempt.
Every echo of giggles holds a truth,
Behind every jab, the joy of our youth.

Through laughter's chaos, the heartbeat sings,
A jagged melody, yet bliss it brings.
For in this garden where humor is tried,
We embrace the thorns, with laughter as our guide.

Whispers of the Thorn

In a garden where cacti dance,
A sarcastic grin takes a chance.
They poke and tease with every glance,
Each thorn a jab in this odd romance.

The roses roll their eyes in glee,
While daisies sip their herbal tea.
Watch out now, they'll poke just three,
And laugh as they flee, oh woe is me!

A cactus with jokes, quite the sight,
Spitting puns through the starry night.
Come join the feast, don't take a bite—
The punchlines are sharp, but oh, what a fright!

In this garden, blooms so absurd,
Every breeze carries a quirky word.
So tiptoe lightly, don't let it be heard,
Lest you fall into laughter, unheard!

Unforgiving Lines

A poet once wrote with a frown,
Each word a thorn in a prickly crown.
He scribbled and scratched, nearly down,
His rhymes rebelling, a comedic clown.

Lines that tangled and wrestled with fate,
They bickered and joked, never late.
With every attempt at something great,
They tripped over wit and laughter's gait.

In corridors where quills take a stand,
Every letter is rude, but oh so grand.
They giggle and poke, go hand in hand,
Turning sweet prose into slapstick land.

So if you find humor in what you compose,
Let your stanzas clown, don't take it close.
Each wobbling line may lead to a dose,
Of laughter so rich, it's like fine prose!

The Edge of Sentiment

On the brink of feeling a bit too much,
Sentiments hover, just out of touch.
They prickle with passion, never a crutch,
A wink and a nudge, oh such is the clutch!

Love notes are scribbled, then crumpled in haste,
Each word a silly, bittersweet taste.
They flirt and evade, a humorous chase,
Spilling out giggles in an awkward embrace.

The jokes they repeat, in love's tangled game,
What's poignant turns punchy, not quite the same.
Every heartfelt whisper fuels the flame,
As laughter and tears entwine in a name.

So tread lightly on feelings, my friend,
For at the edge, sweet foolishness blends.
In the heart of humor, we'll find our trends,
Lively and joyous, where laughter transcends!

A Garden of Complications

Welcome to chaos, a strange little spot,
Where flowers argue what's cold and what's hot.
The daisies bicker, the tulips plot,
Send sunshine to doom, oh what a thought!

Beneath the surface of green, they fight,
Each petal a word in a comedic plight.
Amidst all the blooms, it's a humorous sight,
As nature crackles with laughter so bright.

In tangled vines, a mystery swirls,
The bees buzzing secrets that whirl and twirl.
Every thorn pricks at chaos unfurls,
In this garden of silly, laughter unfurls.

So if you stroll in this perplexing maze,
Prepare for the fun of bewildered blaze.
For in the mix of quirk and crazed,
A garden of giggles forever stays!

Sharp Edges of Rhyme

A poet once tried to write so slick,
His pen slipped away, a mischievous trick.
Words danced on the page, a peculiar sight,
Like hedgehogs in socks, they all took flight.

His rhymes had a bite, sharp as a knife,
Each couplet licked back, full of strange life.
Oh, the joy and the pain, of wielding such art,
Each stanza a puzzle, each line a sharp dart.

With verses that poked and pricked like a rose,
A jest or a jab, no one could suppose.
In laughter we read, and oh how we cried,
At the wounds of his wit, so painfully wide.

Yet through all the chaos, a sweet truth emerged,
In humor's embrace, all our frowns were purged.
For art that can sting is a curious brew,
It tickles and nips, but it's lovely too.

Uneasy Sentences

Words wobbled and jigged, with a mind of their own,
In sentences twisted, like rubber, they'd moan.
Each paragraph shimmied, with odd little hops,
Like a chicken in boots, laughing right off the tops.

A subject went missing, verb lost in the fray,
While adverbs were arguing, much to our dismay.
Punctuation was dancing, in party attire,
Commas were drinking, while periods conspire.

The syntax was stuttering, a sight deemed absurd,
As nouns wore loud hats, and the verbs just slurred.
Oh, the tales that they tell, in their topsy-turvy spree,
With each crooked line, brought a laugh, a glee.

So here's to the chaos, the jumbled delight,
In uneasy sentences, where humor takes flight.
For every twist, turn, and every odd phrase,
Makes us chuckle and grin, in new silly ways.

Thorny Tales

Once upon a time, in a bumpy old book,
Characters grumbled, with each funny look.
They stumbled on plot twists, with each crazy spin,
Like porcupines dancing, let the fun begin.

A villain in sneakers, who tripped on his cape,
Chased heroes in flip-flops, who giggled and scraped.
The rhymes pricked our hearts, much like a small thorn,
Yet laughter erupted, each tale was reborn.

From dragons with hiccups, to fairies who snooze,
The stories grew wild, wrapped in silly shoes.
Oh, the prickly adventures, they took us on flight,
Through thorns made of laughter, under the moonlight.

So gather round, friends, as we tell of these gales,
In the world of thorny, wacky tales.
For every sharp story that leaves us in stitches,
Brings joy to our hearts, and delightful glitches.

Sharp Quills and Silken Threads

A quill scribbled wildly, with threads that were bright,
  Embroidery of words, brought to life in the night.
  Each stitch was a chuckle, each knot a big grin,
    As verses fell soft, like feathers in the wind.

  The fabric of stories was wobbly and bold,
   With colors and patterns, like tales yet untold.
   Laughter intertwined with every thin line,
     Weaving the ridiculous into a design.

  In a tapestry awkward, yet vibrant and warm,
      A parade of oddities began to swarm.
   Quills danced in circles, arms open wide,
    While gluing together what humor implied.

   So let us unite, with our quills and our thread,
    In crafting a laughter, where giggles are bred.
For sharpness can charm, when it makes us all gleam,
 In a world woven fast, where we dream and we beam.

An Overture of Edges

In the garden of words, be aware,
Some leave you prepped, others ensnare.
A cactus might grin, oh so spry,
But it's sharp as a dart flying by.

Bantering tongues, such a riot,
Turning phrases, yet we deny it.
Laughter erupts, then we peek,
At the stitches that snapped, oh so bleak.

With each poke, a jest takes flight,
Jab it with humor, hold on tight.
A sonnet may sting, yet we all sing,
In this prickly garden, let bellies swing.

So come take a stroll on these thorns,
Where giggles grow wild, not forlorn.
We dance on the edge, hearts open wide,
Every slip a joyride, no need to hide.

Vexed Verses

Each line I craft, a puzzle piece,
Some grip you soft, others don't cease.
Words collide, with a comic spit,
Swinging through language, a perfect fit.

A pun's a taunt, ready to tease,
Like dodging raindrops, overly pleased.
Yet with every nuage, a jab does prance,
In this circus of letters, we waltz and dance.

I write with zeal, but it can sting,
As sharp as a bee in early spring.
Chasing the quips, they dart and weave,
With every touch found, we take our leave.

So here's to the joy, the poke and prod,
In each silly line, a gentle nod.
We'll laugh and clack through this lexical maze,
Where pain and jest waltz in a daze.

The Wounded Wordsmith

Once I crafted a tale so bright,
Only to find it hurling in flight.
With leans and bends, my quill took flight,
Creating chaos, what a delight!

Out sprouted verses, a prick in the air,
Exclamation points, everywhere!
With jabs of wit, I soared so high,
But smooth prose slips, why oh why?

Each stanza a giggle, a puzzling heart,
As I pen down mishaps, each one an art.
In the theater of laughter, occasionally stung,
My words do a jig, yet they've all wrung.

So here's to the zingers that backfire too,
With a twist and a chuckle, who knew?
In this wordsmith's realm, I dance and weep,
Crafting blunders that never sleep.

Blunt Realities

Where truth and jest have a playful fight,
A slip of a word can show off the light.
With sharp-witted pens, we carve the thick,
In blunt engagements, humor hits quick.

Talking in circles, a tight-laced bind,
Yet the laughter unfolds, oddly kind.
Reality bites, with a snicker, a jest,
But life's bitter pill is still more than jest.

Through faux pas and flops, we gleefully roam,
In the fields of discourse, we find our home.
With edges that jibe and ricochet bright,
We stumble on words that cause sheer delight.

So hold on to hilarity, let it suffice,
For even in stitch-ups, there's glitter of spice.
In the narrative thorns, we find our embrace,
Laughing through life, at our own fevered pace.

Barbs of Authenticity

In a garden of truth, I tripped on my tongue,
Where honesty dances, all tangled and sprung.
The weeds of confusion, they tickle and poke,
A jab of a joke, with no sign of a yoke.

I wear my quirks like a badge of great pride,
With laughter as armor, I'm ready to glide.
Each twist and each turn, like a prank on the floor,
Who knew honesty could be such a chore?

My expressions are sharper than a cactus's spire,
With metaphors jabbing, I never tire.
The punchlines are scrawny, but woven with glee,
In a bush of lunchboxes, come learn them with me.

So let's toast to the barbs, the jests that we bear,
In the realm of true stories, beware the hot air.
In laughter's embrace, we bare all that we find,
With souls that are pruned, but sweetly entwined.

Fiery Fragments

I wrote a sharp sonnet that sizzles and pops,
With fragments of spice that dance and that hops.
A sprinkle of chaos, a dash of disdain,
Each stanza ignites like a runaway train.

In the oven of humor, I bake them just right,
A pinch of absurdity sparks the delight.
These words, they flambé, with such glorious flair,
Like fireworks bursting, all caught in mid-air.

I threw in some puns, just to raise the heat,
While dangling my thoughts on a spaghetti treat.
A dish full of nonsense, served with a grin,
Who knew that scattered lines could help one to win?

So let's laugh through the ashes, those bits of delight,
In the kitchen of wit, everything's bright.
With flavors exploding, the feast is now set,
In fiery fragments, arise from your fret.

The Rough Road to Poetics

On the winding road, where the oddballs reside,
Each line's a new bump, I cling to my pride.
With potholes of puns and detours of rhyme,
I trip over humor, what's wrong with this time?

There's gravel of giggles, and chuckles abound,
With shrubs of absurdity sprouting around.
I navigate chaos, my compass a laugh,
Taking wrong turns in the poetic half.

The roundabouts twist, and the signs lead me wrong,
Yet I keep humming my off-key song.
In the clutches of quirk, I swagger and sway,
The road's always bumpy, but hey, that's okay!

So gather your maps and join in this ride,
On the rough road of verse, my humor's my guide.
With jokes as the fuel, we'll travel quite far,
Embracing the mess, that's the joy of the car!

Citric Paths

Along the citrus trail, I skip with a grin,
Juicy jests dangling from every thick skin.
With lemons of laughter, and oranges too,
A fruit salad of wit, come see what we brew!

In the orchard of quirks, the sunshine is bright,
Let's squeeze all our troubles till they're out of sight.
With zest in our hearts, we frolic and leap,
In the tang of the citrus, our joy runs deep.

Each vine whispers secrets, in breezy delight,
As we skedaddle through foliage, oh what a sight!
We toss in a giggle, we catch a ripe laugh,
In this grove of humor, let's find our own path.

So let's paint our days in these tangy hues,
With citric creations that spark and amuse.
Together we'll wander, with zest and with cheer,
On citric paths paved with laughter, my dear!

The Edge of Wit

Sharp jests dance in the air,
Like hedgehogs with flair.
They poke and they prod,
With laughter's odd nod.

Wit can be brash,
A playful, wild clash.
Tickling minds with a tease,
Like bees that won't cease.

Sarcasm, a thorn,
In jest, we are worn.
Yet smiles bloom wide,
With humor as guide.

So let's giggle and snort,
In this quirky sport.
With wordplay so spry,
We'll give wit a try.

Quills and Quarrels

In a garden of spines,
Where argument shines.
Quills ruffle and sway,
As we banter and play.

The blossoms all argue,
With debates that ensue.
Petty squabbles and jest,
Who's the quirkiest guest?

Each flower has flair,
With humor laid bare.
A comical duel,
In this botanical school.

Yet friendship can bloom,
In the midst of the room.
With laughter as glue,
We quill with a view.

The Unruly Bouquet

A bouquet of odd sorts,
With laughter retorts.
Petals that tease and tug,
Like a cheeky little bug.

Roses roll their eyes,
In a bedlam of sighs.
Daisies giggle aloud,
A playful, raucous crowd.

Sunflowers give cheek,
Their humor at peak.
Tulips poke fun,
'Oh, who's number one?'

In the chaos of cheer,
Friendship draws near.
An unruly bouquet,
That dances at play.

Petals of Dissent

Petals flutter and clash,
In a humorous flash.
With whimsy in tow,
They dance to and fro.

All the flowers unite,
In a whimsical fight.
Chasing shadows with glee,
In this flower spree.

Arguments bloom like sun,
In the laughter we've spun.
Each petal a cheeky,
Flirtatious little streaky.

Yet still they must share,
Their humor laid bare.
In petals of dissent,
The joy is well spent.

Deflation of Flattery

Oh, compliments can soar so high,
Like balloons that kiss the sky.
But with a pin, they swiftly drop,
Leaving us with quite a flop.

Inflated words can mess with heads,
Like jelly beans in tangled threads.
Yet truth sometimes feels just like a joke,
As laughs fly free with every poke.

The mirror lies, it's plain to see,
As I'm flatter than a raft at sea.
So I'll survive with ego small,
And just enjoy this awkward fall.

When praise is light, I float away,
Yet deeper thoughts bring shades of gray.
So here's a cheer for failure's grace,
In wobbly sways, we find our place.

Penning with Punctures

With sharp words dipped in sneaky ink,
A writer's pen can make you think.
Punctuation might stab your brain,
Leaving you chuckling at the pain.

Commas wiggle, semicolons frown,
As I trip over these ups and downs.
Each exclamation starts a riot,
While periods force a hush so quiet.

The words collide, yet dance with glee,
In a world so absurd, it's hard to see.
With every slash, there's a laugh or two,
We pen our tales, all poking through.

So let your thoughts be sharp and bright,
And puncture flaws with all your might.
For in this game of verbal play,
The joy's found in the fray.

The Harsh Constellation

Stars can twinkle, but not quite say,
How badly jokes can go astray.
They light up the night, but much like us,
They can sting quick and create a fuss.

Galaxies hold their witty charms,
Yet when they joke, they come with harms.
A cosmic giggle can start a mess,
Leaving us in a humorous stress.

Each comet trails a biting pun,
While gravity weighs tons of fun.
Orbiting tales in a clumsy dance,
The harshest jabs make us lose our pants.

So let's toast to the stars above,
Crafting laughs we thoroughly love.
In this dark velvet cloak we wear,
We find our light in cosmic care.

The Spiny Branches

In a garden where giggles grow,
Beneath the thorns, the punchlines flow.
Spines twisting up like tangled thoughts,
Prickling laughter, that's what we've sought.

Branches stretch with cheeky grins,
While laughter darts like mischievous pins.
The blooms, oh yes, are sweet and bright,
But watch those thorns, they bite with delight.

Each twist leads to a knotty laugh,
Finding joy in the spiky path.
For florals may wrap their prickly arms,
Yet hearts unite in their odd charms.

So roam the ways of this wild patch,
Where joy and pain make the perfect catch.
With spiny branches reaching wide,
Together we'll dance, side by side.

www.ingramcontent.com/pod-product-compliance
Lightning Source LLC
Chambersburg PA
CBHW051639160426
43209CB00004B/710